Make Money Now!

Build An Online Business Using The internet

By Sandy Murray

CONTENTS

Cover Page
Make money Now!

1	Introduction	Pg # 3
2	Introduction To The Internet	Pg # 6
3	What Is an Online Business?	Pg # 8
4	Identify What You Want To Pursue	Pg # 10
5	Focus on Building Your Business	Pg # 12
6	Develop A Monetization Plan	Pg # 14
7	Different Types Of Online Businesses	Pg # 16
8	Summary	Pg # 32
9	Tired Of The Mundane Rat Race	Pg # 37
10	Some General Tips	Pg # 38

Introduction

If you want to start an online business, you've come to the right place, or if you want to make your current online business more profitable, you've come to the right place.

We will be start at the very beginning, and it's okay if you don't know anything about online business.

Having an online business is not for everyone. But in order to judge whether it's a good fit for you, we first must define what an online business is.

My personal definition: It's a business which is conducted primarily on the internet.

The fact is that it takes hard work to build a business, and there are certain abilities that will greatly increase your chances of success.

The more TIME you can devote to it the better, but don't let a lack of time stop you. If you can only devote a small amount of time at first, that's okay.

You simply need to commit to 3 things.

1.) Be willing to be a marketer;

2.) Like computers and the internet;

3.) Be willing and able to learn (and I know it will take work).

Take some time and be honest with yourself (and don't WORRY about WHAT you'll need to learn - that's what I'm here for, and I'll guide you through the entire process.)

If you are confident in those three things, then I'd say you meet the basic requirements for being able to start an online business. Now you're ready to move onto the next step, in which we'll explore several different types of online businesses.

Introduction To The Internet

The internet is one of the greatest tools for any business. With the growth of global networks and technology, the internet has connected the world into one large market place ripe for exploitation. The internet has gone through transformations since its inception in the late 1990s. With the tremendous growth in technology, we now have access to information from all over the world at our fingertips.

It has greatly changed how we do things, and has led to the creation of many jobs.

The internet has influenced how we work, eat and shop, and has created trade niches that were never there before. With the boom of the internet and social media, a new category of entrepreneurship has arisen, and employers are looking to engage you.

To really utilize the benefits if the internet, you need a network connection and a computer or smart phone that can be connected.

What Is An Online Business?

This is a job that uses the internet to sell a product or a service. Online commerce can also have a physical location too. Some of them can only done only through the web. For instance, a freelance writer is hired by people who barely know him to write articles for them. You need to build a relationship with the other party to make it work.

There is a ton of money to be made using the web. These businesses offer an unmatched opportunity to engage your audience worldwide with only a computer and internet connection.

Starting and growing a business, however, takes time and dedication.

When choosing which work to do, choose something you are good at and focus on your strengths. There are a few things you can do while starting out on building your business.

Identify What You Want To Pursue

Choose your trade according to your strengths and knowledge. Many successful online business owners succeed because they pursued what they love to do. When you do what you love, you will push through until you grow. Will starting a job online compliment your day job and give you access to a bigger audience? Is the plan to grow your website and quit your day job, or is it a hobby you are pursuing?

When you go into an area of work you have training in, you get the upper hand because you can provide the service yourself rather than hire someone else to do it for you.

For example, if you don't know how to code, you can't build a website; thus, you will need to contract a professional who does.

You will need to set up an account on social media or develop a website that will be where you connect to and look for jobs on the web. You can set up a blog or an easy website with free apps found on the net. Alternatively, if you can afford to, get a web designer to create a professionally done site for you.

Focus on Building Your Business

Your business won't pick up and make you million in only a few weeks' time. Focus on growing a following and making the right connections in the community. Utilize social media to connect with your target viewers. Do your research and learn from the mistakes of those who went before you.

The building phase can take a significant amount of time and effort. Put together a rich portfolio that sells itself to future clients. Find a mentor who can give you unbiased advice and help you when you get stuck.

Remember, this is just like any other type of work.

Don't give in to disappointment if things don't work out right away. Keep at it, and with dedication your things will pick up.

Develop A Monetization Plan

When the business has started growing and is generating income it's time to implement your plan to generate and sustain that income. Make a financial plan that will guide your business. Have a way to monitor expenses and how much sales you are making. This way you can monitor your progress and take measures to help you expand.

Set up the appropriate accounts where transactions can be made. Use online payments methods such as PayPal as they have less charges.

Once your business starts supporting itself, and not already done, it's a good idea to upgrade to a professional site that is well presented to consumers. It's always a good idea to start with what you have, then grow. Don't invest all your hard-earned savings in your business. Take advantage of the free resources when starting or invest wisely to get your website situated.

Different Types Of Online Businesses

Starting and growing an online venture is not easy. There is a lot of competition selling a product or a service similar to yours. Some businesses may not require any expertise and are easier than others to start. With this in mind, the following five online ideas will get you started.

1. SEO Consultant

SEO (Search Engine Optimization) is a great tool in the market and has huge potential, but it helps if you are knowledgeable in platforms like Google Analytics.

Many companies are looking to increase their presence online and through a SEO their clients can find them easily. Educate your clients on the power of a SEO to help transform their websites into a more SEO friendly property. With your experience, you can teach them how to read and use their analytics data the right way, how to properly use keywords, and show them various ways that content can be written to attract more traffic.

Your website is your tool of the trade; use it well in order to get more clients.

Then you and your clients can decide whether you should do the teaching online or visit their offices. Make sure you hire a lawyer to draft a business contract to use when you get new clients.

Ensure that you have clear terms of engagement. When you have a signed contract, this is evidence that a business transaction has taken place and the client is obligated to pay. In cases where clients don't pay, you can sue them for monies owing.

As you keep on growing, more lucrative businesses will come your way. Make sure to build a positive reputation and offer the best service to your clients. You can also write and publish e-books as you gain more clients and a wider following. You will only thrive when you put effort in your work. Don't look for shortcuts or get rich schemes

2. Freelance Writer

This s a great online job that can be done from the comfort of your home. Writers are in great demand on the web. More establishments are hiring writers using this method rather than hiring full time staff. If you have a good command of writing, you can make a great deal of money by writing online.

From students who are too lazy to do their homework to professional papers and websites that need new content all the time, the work is readily available for a person who can write well and quickly. According to the freelance job listing website, freelance.com, tech services, content creation, and web design are popular fields for contract work. There is also a lot of demand for good photography, so if you are good with a camera, take photos of interesting places and people and sell them online.

It's easy to get started. Scour the web looking for people needing writers.

There are many topics for you to write about so you'll be able to get something that interests you. Get a comfortable desk and chair, a strong network connection, and a laptop and get started.

The secret to being an accomplished writer lies in being disciplined and delivering projects on time. If your work is good, better paying assignments will come. There are many people working as content writers and making a good income using the internet.

Online Clothing Store

Fashion is ever-changing and people are always investing in the newest trends. If you are selling at the right price, someone will definitely buy. Identify which market segment you want to specialize in, be it women's or men's or baby's clothes. Set up a very appealing website and display your merchandise with quality in mind. Propose to sell quality items because that will create repeat transactions. Invest in a good camera or employ a professional to take the photographs.

All you need is a web-hosting service with an integrated shopping cart feature or with e-commerce software, and your store will be operational in no time.

Use established platforms like eBay and Shoopfly to set up a shop, and then start selling clothes or handmade materials in a matter of days. You can even work with vendors to ship products to customers on your behalf, which means you don't need to own a lot of inventory.

Use the powerful social media platforms like Instagram and Facebook to market yourself.

As you gain more followers, this will translate to money through sales from your store. You don't need to have a physical address to start a clothing store online. You can work from with a laptop and internet connection.

4. Blogging

If you love telling stories and writing, then this may be your next thing.

This venture is best suited for folks who enjoy communicating about a particular subject. From personal blogs to professional topics, blogs are capable of earning a great deal of money.

You can write just about anything that interests you – fashion, traveling, sports cars, parenting, technology – the list is endless. Just make sure you are passionate about the topic you choose and make it interesting and of high quality.

You don't need to be an expert in your field. As long as you are passionate about it, once you start you can grow your knowledge as you go along.

You don't need to invest in high-tech gadgets when you begin; use what you have to convey your message.

A good camera and editing skills will help you produce high quality images for your blog.

It may take a while before you make any money but when traffic increases, the money will starts trickling in. Use Ad-Sense (Google's ad revenue sharing plan) to make residual income. When you keep growing, opportunities for sponsorship's will arise.

As with any business, utilize social media to expose yourself to your readers. Make use of YouTube to attract those readers who prefer watching than reading. Most of the accomplished bloggers started small and grew over the years to make six-figure incomes. The trick here is to be consistent. Have a schedule of posting that your followers know about. Remind them there is a new blog post through your accounts.

5. Social Media Consultant

Many corporations are looking to appoint someone to manage their social media accounts. Larger firms delegate to an agency or employ staff to manage their online accounts, but up-and coming or medium sized firms often have to handle their own social media marketing. They usually hire someone to manage their social media accounts because they understand the importance of an online presence at an agreed fee or commission.

Remember, all you need is a laptop or smart phone to get started as a social media specialist.

You can help clients expand their presence on the web and help them engage with their customers online. Here you will be in charge of posting news and bulletins, and answering questions asked by customers.

You need to have people skills to fully engage with the followers and interact with them behalf of your client.

If you enjoy meeting new people and interacting with them, then this job may be the right fit for you.

6. Web Designer

To work as a web designer, expertise is needed. You need to know how to code in order to design a website. Make sure your work is outstanding because potential customers will review your previous work before hiring you. If you know HTML and have a good eye for design, you can launch a service to create attractive, easy-to-use websites for businesses. You need to work on your reputation to deliver quality work at the agreed time.

Nothing kills a budding online business faster than bad reviews.

Have a well-put portfolio to display to your capabilities to potential clients. Let your good work do the talking for you. Organizations are willing to pay top dollar to have the best website money can buy. Put your skills to good use by creating extraordinary websites for your clients who want to take their online presence to the next level. Build a comprehensive portfolio, and then create your own website to illustrate and attract a steady stream of clients.

Summary

The growth of the internet has led to a rise in online entrepreneurs who want to utilize the web to get rich. There are many good and bad web surfers out there. There are many scams online. When setting out with your business, do your research and work with people who have good reviews and reputations. It's possible to get scammed, so be on the lookout for people wanting to make a quick buck out of you.

Do your due diligence before paying for any services online. Make sure the work is delivered before parting with your money.

Some people will want to get good work done without paying for your effort.

Follow all the legal requirements needed in your country when setting up an online store. Register the name of your company and prepare all the other legal papers you need. Make sure you pay your taxes on time to avoid legal action. Copyright laws apply for all businesses, so make sure you are within the limits.

Competition is very high in the web. To counter this, make sure your product or service is of the best quality and reasonably priced because customers are always looking for the next, best deal at the lowest price.

Always produce content that is authentic and unique to you. Don't plagiarize another writer's work. Make sure to produce information that will help the person reading it. This way, you remain relevant.

Making money won't happen overnight. Exercise patience and work hard at doing your job. Just like any other business, it will follow a similar curve and may take you months, if not years, to see any significant money coming your way. You need to keep working at what you're doing so success will find you.

Its better you keep your daytime job as you work on building your online one. This way you can keep earning your keep until your trade can sustain you. Not all online businesses will pick up and go on to be successful. If yours does fail, this is okay; go on and work on your next idea.

Read about people who succeeded in their line of work and learn from their mistakes.

People do well when they put effort into what they are doing.

Read books to help you improve your knowledge on what you are doing. Discipline is key when you plan to start your business. Do your research on technological improvements that can aid and promote your business.

Do not underestimate the power of social sites such as Facebook, Twitter and Instagram. Over 2.5 billion people are on social media sites. When used properly, these sites are crucial for hunting for potential clients. Take advantage of it to grow.

To learn more about starting a Home Based Business you can check out my YouTube Channel here.

[How to start a home based business](https://goo.gl/rH00Kx)

https://goo.gl/rH00Kx

Tired Of The Mundane Rat Race

If you're tired of the mundane rat race and you want more freedom and control over the hours you work, why not start a home based business?

You need to ask yourself if you have an entrepreneurial mindset and the dedication required to start and maintain a home based business full time. Also take a look at your skills and interests to get an idea of what kind of business you will have.

It also helps to have money saved up before taking the plunge to assist you during emergencies. Here is additional advice on starting a home based business.

Some General Tips

Start the process by choosing a business name that is unique enough to stand out yet one that is still relevant to what you are selling. The business name should also be memorable to potential customers.

You should research your city and state laws regarding a home based business, and you will need to obtain any required permits and licenses. Secure funding by creating a detailed and realistic business plan. The business plan should include the nature of the business, how you plan to promote it, and projected sales over the next five years.

Understand Your Industry Well

Before you start a home based business you should research and understand the industry that your business will be focused on.

If you are creating homeschooling curriculum e books for families, you can attend some homeschooling conventions to get an idea of what the latest home school curriculum trends are. While at the conventions, interview some home school families to see which needs you can fill through your business.

Know The Risks Of A Home Based Businesses

You're excited about the benefits of a home based business but do you know some of the risks involved? As you spend more time building the business, you might decide to quit your regular job but then you will lose significant income. There is also the risk of not earning adequate funds when you first start the business. Your work-life balance might not be the best at times when running a home based business, and sometimes your family might feel neglected because you're spending so much time on your business.

I Have A Full Time Job. How Can I Start A Home Based Business?

Start by setting realistic goals on how much you can do to get the home based business business off the ground. Maybe you can spend your days off pitching your ideas to potential clients if you are building a freelance writing business. And when you have vacation time, you can meet with businesspersons who might need blog posts and press releases on a weekly or daily basis.

Seek out loved ones and friends as your first customers and if they are satisfied, they will refer you to new customers.

Cutting Down On Expenses While Running A Home Based Business

One way to do this is by taking advantage of the tax deductions that are available to home based business owners.

Some tax deductions you can claim on your tax return include car expenses, insurance for business purposes, supplies used to run your home business such as a desktop computer, and other kinds of costs associated with running a home based business.

Another way to cut down on business expenses is to purchase office supplies at a wholesaler for an affordable price.

Organization Is Key

A home based businesses involve a lot of paperwork, inventory and office equipment and supplies, it is important to stay organized as much as possible. Purchase a planner for writing down due dates of projects for clients, meeting dates with suppliers, and for managing your business expenses. Utilize spreadsheet programs such as Excel and Access to document financial information. Also get rid of the digital clutter by removing unwanted emails from your in box.

In conclusion, home based businesses allow you to earn a stable income while still remaining at home with your family. You should take note of your strengths, weaknesses, skills and interests before starting your business and you need to meet with an accountant who is familiar with local and state laws regarding home based windows. Promote the business by creating social media accounts, writing a regular blog about how your business meets a customer's needs, and giving out fliers and business cards at local trade shows.

DEDICATION

For my wife, Gillian – for her love, and her undying support and encouragement of my crazy choices in my life.

ABOUT THE AUTHOR

I enjoyed writing this book and believe it may help others build an online business. Read what you need and leave the rest - or pass it on to a friend.

www.ingramcontent.com/pod-product-compliance
Lightning Source LLC
Chambersburg PA
CBHW041205180526
45172CB00006B/1204